The Dolls' House

by **FAITH BRADFORD**

SMITHSONIAN INSTITUTION PRESS
Washington, D.C. 1977

Foreword: How the House Was Created

The Dolls' House was designed by Faith Bradford, the author of this account of the Doll family and their home, in the early 1900s. It is one room deep in order to show completely the contents of each room, but a hallway running the entire length of each floor—and seen through the doorways—gives a feeling of depth and reality.

The collection of furnishings grew from those in a four-room doll house inherited by Miss Bradford from a much older sister in about the year 1887. The only article from the original house is a lamp without its globe, standing on the cedar chest in the attic.

Some of the pieces were in other doll houses that Miss Bradford played with as a child, but most were collected in later years. Many came from Washington, D. C., including the furniture in Robin and Christopher Doll's room, which was bought at a toy store where Abraham Lincoln had bought toys for his little son Tad. Some of the miniature pieces were ordered from other parts of the United States, and a very few came from foreign countries.

Most of the rugs, window curtains, and drapes were made by Miss Bradford or her friends. There are many "contrived" pieces. The ceiling light in the sewing room, for example, is an oil can; the shades of the standing lamps are cut-down cups; and the "linoleum" is oilcloth.

Most of the books in the bookcase were made by cutting to suitable size strips of grooved wood used for holding leads for pencils. Flat matches were then inserted in the grooves, and the whole was painted to resemble individual books, or books in sets. The books between bookends on the drum table in the library are actual printed books.

It is possible to mention here the origins and histories of only a few of the other articles. The ivory sea lion on a shelf of the whatnot in the drawing room came from the Bering Strait region. A portrait of Miss Bradford's grandfather, a tinted cut in an old daguerreotype frame, hangs above the mantel in the library. The cabinet of curios in the parlor came, already filled, from Mexico. And a tiny china doll, more than 100 years old, is held by Lucy in the day nursery.

The house and furnishings were created to an approximate scale of 1 inch to 1 foot. The house is 4½ feet high, 7½ feet wide, and about 1½ feet deep.

MARGARET BROWN KLAPTHOR

Curator of political history,
National Museum of History and Technology,
Smithsonian Institution

The Family of Doll

Who are the people that live in this house? What are their interests? What servants do they have? To enter into the spirit of the Dolls' home in about the year 1905, let us meet the inhabitants.

Peter Doll, the head of the family, is about 35 years old. He is successful financially, with perhaps an inheritance as a solid background. He is a man of integrity, well regarded in his community, much loved by his family. He enjoys social life, as is indicated by his gracious drawing room; is well educated, witness his well-stocked library; has an interest in music; is something of a student in his own study; and is interested in sports, by token of the trophy on his desk and his bicycle.

Mr. Doll has a charming wife and ten happy children. At the moment, he stands at his study door, about to enter the library where his hound waits to welcome him.

Rose (Washington) Doll, growing matronly in her repeated happy motherhood, still retains her charm at 31. She has lost none of her social ease while acquiring the skills needed to direct her large household. She and Mr. Doll have many interests in

Mr. Doll

common—in social life, in cultural attainments, and the sincere practice of their religion. Mrs. Doll may be seen in the doorway of the parents' bedroom, where she is reassuring herself of the safety and comfort of the youngest children, the 3-month-old identical twins, Jimmy and Timmy.

Fortunately, the ten children are all healthy, although it could be wished that Christopher had fewer colds. Ann's delicate look is deceptive, since she is never ill. Peter Jr. is 11, and Alice is 10; and both have exceptionally happy dispositions. Dainty little Ann is 7; responsible Robin is 6; and Lucy and Carol, the unidentical but inseparable twins, are 5. Carol is a true blonde, Lucy an ash blonde. Christopher fancies himself a horseman, although he has never seen a movie nor watched TV. He is 4 years old, and a bit tall for his age. Plump David is 18 months old, and none is sturdier than he. Nurse has her hands full watching him.

Robin, 6

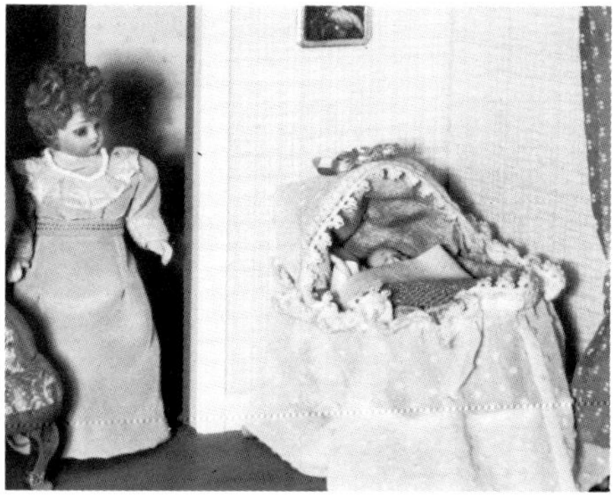

Mrs. Doll with Jimmy and Timmy, 3 months

Christopher, 4

Alice, 10

David, 18 months, with Nurse McNab

Lucy and Carol, 5

Ann, 7, with her cat, Mrs. Peerie

Peter Jr., 11

Grandfather Doll

Grandfather and Grandmother Doll are honored visitors now occupying the guest room, as is evidenced by their much-traveled trunk. Dr. Sylvester Doll may seem older than his 67 years, but in his life of medical service he has not spared himself. His wife, Serena (Bradstreet) Doll, is glad to have him take one of his rare vacations. Except for her pretty white hair, Grandmother does not look her 63 years. She is quietly playing solitaire now, with her watchful collie, Mac, beside her. Grandfather has just refreshed himself with a hot bath, and is entering the bedroom.

Grandmother Doll with Mac, her collie

The Service in the House

Gadsby, the butler

Mrs. Doll plans and personally directs the running of her household, and she has competent help.

Elspeth McNab, of good Scots parentage, had her first nursing experience with Peter Jr. when he was just a month old. She has been with the family ever since, and no child in her care has ever had a serious mishap. Right now, Nurse McNab is in the night nursery, about to put little David to bed after his supper.

We see Gadsby, the butler, in his pantry inspecting the silver to be used in a short while at dinner. Gadsby might be serving in a family of greater wealth, but he finds the Doll household exactly suited to his taste. The Dolls require good service, which he appreciates, and, since they do quite a bit of formal entertaining, he has a chance to show his talents. Moreover, in the Dolls' service he met Abby Woodthrop, who is now Mrs. Gadsby.

Woodthrop (Mrs. Gadsby), the parlormaid

Martha, the cook

She is known as Woodthrop in the household, where she plans to continue serving as parlormaid until she becomes an expert seamstress, her present study. Eventually she hopes to take the place of Mrs. Doll's dressmaker, who comes twice a year to work in the sewing room but who is not present at this time.

Christina Young, the chambermaid, has been with the Dolls for only a short time, but she is living up to her reputation for efficiency and energy. Today, armed with bucket and mop, she is moving from room to room, leaving each one in spotless condition. Right now, she can be seen leaving the children's bathroom.

Martha Roots, a queen among cooks, has the right understanding of a roast of beef, and a light hand with pastry. At the moment she is closing the doors of the icebox after a delivery of ice and milk.

Pets

Spot

Jolly

Not long ago Mrs. Doll made a feeble gesture toward reducing the number of household pets, but it came to nothing.

Mr. Doll's hound, Spot,is in the library, probably anticipating his master's entry, or perhaps hoping to get away with a nap in the chair before he comes in.

Mrs. Doll's springer spaniel, Maydew, is waiting for his mistress in the family parlor. Mrs. Doll thinks that Maydew is the cleverest dog in the house, and he probably agrees with her.

Peter Jr. and his ferocious-looking (but really amiable) bull dog, Teddy, have a case of mutual adoration, but the boy's white rats are rather special, too. The largest rat is Henri, who came from France. He is on top of the cage in Peter Jr.'s room. The other rats are on the floor. They are Marco from Italy, Sun from China, and Dorado from Mexico. Peter Jr. can tell them apart, but nobody else can.

Alice's pet is Lady Grey, a beautiful cat who loves to lie on the windowsill in her mistress's room. Alice is there petting her now.

Ann's cat, Mrs. Peerie, usually is not allowed in the night nursery, but tonight Ann has permission to show Mrs. Peerie to

David before he goes to bed. David is too young to have a special pet of his own.

Robin, like his older brother, shares his love with several pets. Jolly, his fox terrier, is always good for a romp, and his rabbits, Mr. and Mrs. Whitey, are a lot of fun, too. The rabbits spend most of their time in a hutch in the backyard, but right now they are with Robin and Jolly in Christopher's and Robin's room.

Teddy

Sam and Nip

Sam, Christopher's wire-haired terrier who was named for a favorite grocery boy, likes nothing better than to beat Nip, Lucy's kitten, to the drinking dish in the laundry. Nip hoped there would be milk in the dish tonight, but there was only water; nevertheless, she is arching her back at Sam, who is at the dish near the washing machine.

Carol's kitten, Tuck, is about to take a drink from a dish in the day nursery, where there is seldom a dog around to cause a dispute.

Each child in the Doll family is responsible for taking care of his own pet or pets. There is some grown-up supervision of such duties, but it isn't conspicuous. Even little Christopher takes part in caring for the pets. He keeps the water dishes clean and full.

Grandmother Doll's collie, Mac, is a guest pet right now. He is a quiet dog of great dignity and loyalty, and he never makes any trouble among the other pets.

Nurse looks after the canary, Minnie, whose cage hangs in a window of the day nursery, and Woodthrop takes care of the goldfish in the parlor. The fish are named Goldie, Wiggle, and Dart, but no one can tell them apart.

Mr. Doll says there are not to be *any* more pets, not even a pollywog.

The Rooms in the House

The Dining Room

The Dolls' dining room has a green embossed wallpaper, white curtains, and red draperies with red tie-backs. The furniture is "weathered" oak, popular at the beginning of the 20th century, probably as a revolt against the ornate Victorian style.

The globe hanging over the dining table has a metallic fringe, and it was the accepted type of dining room light fixture of the

The Dining Room

The Butler's Pantry

The Kitchen

time. Cut glass, such as displayed in the corner cupboard, was found in almost every household of the day. The spoon holder on the serving table was beginning to be frowned upon as "Victorian," and the Dolls will probably relegate it to the attic soon.

The swinging door on the right leads to the butler's pantry.

In the hallway at the back of the dining room is a pedestal that holds a red jar. There is an oriental rug on the floor of the hall. These furnishings may be seen through the portieres, which are red.

The Butler's Pantry

The butler's pantry is painted in the usual rather drab color of the period. If the waffle iron is a recent innovation, the convenient sink is a later one, and it is Gadsby's delight. The stepladder chair brings the top shelves of the large cupboard within easy reach.

The Kitchen

The kitchen is a large room. The stove is a coal-and-gas combination. Some of the utensils are still lying about because Martha has just finished baking some bread and biscuits, which may be seen on the table. The swinging door on the right leads to the pantry.

The Pantry

The Laundry Room

The Drawing Room

The Pantry

In this room are an icebox, shelves for storing food, an ice-cream freezer, a picnic or shopping hamper, a churn, and cleaning equipment.

When the ice-cream freezer is used, the chore of turning its crank will be allotted to one of the children, and the lucky one will be rewarded by being allowed to lick the dasher when the cream is frozen.

There aren't many canned goods on the shelves because in the Dolls' day there weren't many foods sold that way. Down in the cellar there probably are shelf after shelf of pickles and jams and jellies, "put up" at home.

In the niche in the right-hand corner of the room are several pieces of cleaning equipment—the exciting new "Hoover," a carpet sweeper, and the humble broom.

In the hallway at the rear are a baby carriage, in which Jimmy and Timmy take their daily ride, and a stroller, which is David's personal chariot.

The Laundry Room

The Dolls have up-to-date apparatus in the laundry room, but the electric iron has not done away with the "sadiron" that may be heated on the little oil stove when the electric power fails, as it does quite often.

Mr. Doll's bicycle is leaning against the wall in the hallway behind the laundry room.

The Drawing Room

The wallpaper in the drawing room has gilt lines that show faintly on an ecru background. Some touch of gilt usually was found in formal rooms of the period, but wallpaper with gloomy solid gilt was being replaced gradually as rooms were repapered.

The curtains are the proper lace ones, and the window shade has the tassels suitable for a formal room. The gold-trimmed

The Library

green velvet drapes are matched by the portieres at the archway to the hall.

The mahogany furniture in this room has come to the Dolls through the heritage of several generations.

The bearskin rug is at home in this room, as is the curio cabinet with its many sentimental treasures and objects picked up in the family's travels.

One of the special treasures of this room is an original oil painting of a vase of flowers. It hangs on the right wall, over the love seat.

The "front hall" is seen through the archway. Below the large mirror—useful for the arriving or departing guests—is a table on which lie a silver card tray and a rather carelessly left umbrella. Beneath the table is a large white jardiniere that once held a "rubber tree," a favorite houseplant of the 1890s.

The Library This is the largest room in the house. Its blue striped wallpaper provides a good background for more inherited furniture, notably the two breakfronts and the Winthrop desk. This room is much in use, with comfortable chairs and many books.

In the hall, beyond the red velvet portieres, may be seen the telephone and its stand, with a pad for messages and a pencil—tied, lest it stray away. The telephone book is there, too, and a handy small chair for those who enjoy long conversations. On the floor is a gay red-and-gold mat.

The Study This room is Mr. Doll's particular domain. Here he has his own bookcase of books, his much-used desk and chair, and his typewriter.

Through the doorway to the hall can be seen a valuable oriental carving on the wall. There is a Mexican rug on the hall floor.

The Study

The Parlor

The Parlor The Dolls entertain formally in the drawing room, but here in the parlor, with its old Victorian furniture, they enjoy informality.

The wallpaper in the parlor has a green background, but the roses scattered over it match the ecru draperies over the lace curtains. The window shade, like the one in the drawing room, has a tasseled pull.

The chessmen have been set up for an evening game between Mr. Doll and Grandfather Doll.

The goldfish swim ceaselessly in their tank atop the metal stand.

An ancestral portrait, in a gilt frame, hangs on the wall in the hallway, and a Mexican rug lies in the hall just outside the parlor door.

The Guest Room Grandmother and Grandfather are temporary occupants of the guest room. The trunk belongs to them, so it is not normally part of the room's furniture.

The carefully crocheted bedspread was Grandmother's work. She likes to crochet, and she brought some wools with her on this trip. You can see them on the lowboy on the left wall.

The inherited furniture in this room long antedates even the grandparents' generation, but it has been preserved with loving care. In this room the color of the violet draperies is repeated in the border of the rather neutral wallpaper.

If evening fires are to be laid in the other fireplaces, there will be one in the guest room, too, but the entire house is heated through registers. The furnace is in the cellar.

A soft carpeting of old-gold color runs the length of the hallway on the second floor. In the hall outside the guest room is a table that now holds a gilt metal vase with some gay flowers.

The Guest Bathroom

The Guest Room

The Guest Bathroom

This is one of three bathrooms in the Dolls' house. Most homes of this period had only one bathroom, and many houses had two bathrooms, but only a few had three.

Mr. Doll has been particular about having the plumbing in his house as modern as possible. He remembers the bathtubs when he was a little boy. They were zinc affairs, enclosed in wooden cases.

The Parents' Bedroom

The Sewing Room

The Parents' Bathroom

The Sewing Machine

The Sewing Room

The sewing room is equipped for the family's needs. The sewing machine, which is operated by a foot treadle, has been inherited by Mrs. Doll. The lid of the sewing basket stands open on a stand next to the sewing machine. On the opposite side of the small room is a wooden sewing box whose "house-top" lids open on each side. Behind the box stands a dress-form that is used by the seamstress who comes twice a year.

The glass-doored cabinet holds a supply of dress material. The large object standing partly behind the cabinet is a lapboard, on which the seamstress places her sewing materials when she works by hand.

In the hallway behind the sewing room is a conveniently placed old white-painted settle on which loads of linen and blankets often lie on their way to and from the linen closet.

The Parents' Bathroom

The parent Dolls' bathroom is much like the guest bathroom, but it is bigger. Mr. Doll's shaving stand is in a corner.

The Parents' Bedroom

Blue wallpaper covers the walls of the large and comfortable bedroom that serves not only for the parent Dolls but also for the 3-month-old twins, Jimmy and Timmy. No one has suggested that such young babies should sleep in a room by themselves.

While Mrs. Doll may have had good luck with her children, she has not omitted taking care of them, too. She is now standing in the doorway, taking a look at the babies.

Mr. Doll's bureau is as neat as his wife's dressing table. But he left a pair of shoes on the floor in front of the bureau.

On the wall in the hallway behind Mrs. Doll is a picture of a country cottage where the Dolls spent a happy summer the year before Lucy and Carol were born. Peter Jr. so enjoyed the garden at that cottage that he wished they lived there all the time.

The Doll House in the Day Nursery

The Day Nursery

At the moment, the day nursery is unusually serene. Lucy and Carol are playing quietly on the floor, and, although he is on his rocking horse, Christopher is not shouting and waving a gun. The twins are playing with dolls and a set of china furniture. The doll in the blue silk dress that Lucy is holding was new in about 1843, and the china furniture dates from about 1873.

There are many toys in the room. A game of checkers has been set up, and there is a doll house in the left corner. The shelves in the other corner hold books and some dishes from which the smaller children ate their supper of bread and milk only a little while ago. The glass pitcher, the pewter bowls, and the spoons are all washed now, and put away.

Lucy's little white cat, Tuck, is having an evening drink. Soon Tuck will be taken downstairs, perhaps to the cellar, for the night; and Minnie, the canary in the cage at the window, will put her head under a wing and go to sleep.

On the wall in the hallway hangs a picture of Mr. Bittenger, a beloved cat that belonged to Miss Bradford, the previous owner of the house.

The Children's Bathroom

The Day Nursery

The Children's Bathroom

Christina has just tidied up the children's bathroom. There are so many children to take baths in this room that Mrs. Doll has put there a "towel horse" that holds many towels. In one corner of the bathroom is a small round tub for the babies. It is still used for David's baths sometimes.

The Night Nursery

The Night Nursery The night nursery has the same neutral wallpaper as the day nursery, but its paper has no gay border, possibly because it would be distracting. The night nursery is a quiet room, immaculate with its white furniture. All the children love the "Madonna of the Chair," the picture that is hanging on the wall.

Four children sleep here now, but soon one of them, Ann, will have a room of her own. David still sleeps in the cradle, which he will soon outgrow. Lucy and Carol sleep in the wider bed, and Ann sleeps in the one that can be seen behind Nurse.

The beds are pretty high, so Lucy and Carol have a little stool that they use for climbing into bed.

When the children are asleep in the night nursery, Nurse or Mother may wish to look in at them without making a light in the room. Then the lamp in the hall, standing on the old marble-topped table, may give enough light. The lamp has been electrified, so it isn't dangerous in case of a pre-bedtime romp. The hallway's floor is entirely carpeted as a safety measure, too.

Nurse's Room

Alice's Room

Nurse's Room Nurse McNab has a cheerful room with golden oak furniture. She is happy to have the old-fashioned washstand set, which is not unlike the one she used in her childhood room in Scotland. She also enjoys using the convenient table, which is equipped for writing letters. In her letters home, Nurse McNab always tells of her affection for the American family.

Alice's Room This pink room would be a delight for any little girl. Mr. Doll gave Alice, his first daughter, a large copy of the picture "Age of Innocence," which is at the right on the wall. Over Alice's bed is a carefully lettered prayer, "Now I Lay Me Down to Sleep."

Just now, Alice is looking out the window and petting her cat, Lady Grey, who likes to lie on the windowsill.

The Attic

The Attic

The raftered attic is filled with many things. These articles include those that have been too recently used to be easily discarded, such as the marble-topped Victorian pieces; inherited treasures such as the hooded cradle, and the flax and spinning wheels; and seasonal items, such as the canoe, lawn mower, and sled. Also, there are some articles that are in need of mending, and they may get it, someday.

The steamer chair is a veteran of travels of cherished memories. The iron deer has been taken from the lawn in the interest of modernization; and the flowers under glass have been removed from the parlor for the same reason. The Christmas wreath is brought down to decorate the house each Christmas season.

The ship in a bottle is fascinating to the children, who sometimes are allowed to play in the attic on a rainy day.

Robin's and Christopher's Room

There are two finished rooms on the attic floor. One belongs to Robin and Christopher. It has golden oak furniture that used to be in Mr. Doll's room when he was a little boy and shared a room with *his* brother.

Most of the boys' toys are in the day nursery, but Christopher keeps his toy stable where he can see it just before the lights are put out. He has a "horse" picture in his room, and Robin has a "rabbit" picture. Both boys have baseball bats that are like those of their big brother, Peter Jr.

Robin's and Christopher's Room

Christopher is playing in the day nursery right now, but Robin is in his room having a good-night session with his rabbits, Mr. and Mrs. Whitey, before he takes them down to their hutch for the night. Robin's fox terrier, Jolly, feels that too much attention is being given these dumb bunnies.

The White Rats

Peter Jr.'s Room Peter Jr. is a very happy fellow, and he also is a responsible "big brother." His parents feel that he will look out for his younger brothers in the next room.

Although he is the oldest in a family of ten children, Peter Jr. still has a few cherished toys about. But he studies faithfully at his desk, where a little Mexican band looks down at him.

Just now Peter Jr. is looking over white rat family. He knows all his rats by name—Henri, Sun, Marco, and Dorado. Teddy, his bull dog, does not share Peter Jr.'s enthusiasm for the rats, but he accepts them.

The Trunk Room The small trunk room under the eaves is visited only when a trip is in prospect. Some late visitor has been a bit careless, though, and left a Paisley shawl dangling under the lid of a trunk.

Peter Jr.'s Room

Alice and Lady Grey

The Significance of the House

Nothing seems to go so rapidly out of mind as the tastes, the sounds, the smells, and the manners of the generation immediately previous to our own. We concern ourselves with the more distant past, with the immediate present, and with the problematic future. Perhaps this attitude could be explained in Freudian terms as a corollary to the oppositions that develop within the immediate family group. Sometimes the bonds of sympathy and appreciation skip over the intervening generation to link grandchild and grandparent in an understanding that eludes the parent and the child. The child can understand and enjoy the world of grandmother—as revealed, for example, in the Bradford Doll House—even if father and mother perhaps cannot.

Miss Faith Bradford—the remarkable woman who created the Bradford Doll House and donated it to the Smithsonian Institution—shared the joys of creation with artists working in other media. Not only did she oversee the construction of the house and personally furnish it, but she filled it with people and with a past. Miss Bradford did not go at this as a contractor might, careful to duplicate exactly specific examples of existing furniture of the early 1900s. The Bradford Doll House is an interpretation of the past, and one must accept it as an interpretation.

Its limitations are those of the artist, whose eye sees some things as important and some as unimportant, who works with toy furniture that may or may not fit to a prearranged scale, and who expresses mood and color and emotion rather than precise scale and measurement. Just as the artist communicates through a medium that may be distorted technically, so did Miss Bradford convey the life of the early 1900s through her interpretation of its household center. In that period the household was a real center; and the house was not a roosting place only, for the times in between trips to the supermarket, the movie house, or the beach. It was not a "machine for living." One did not throw away what was not immediately useful, as there was always a place for it in the attic or in one of the storerooms. Then, life had a continuity that has been partially lost.

It is the world of our grandparents or great grandparents that is communicated by this miniature house and its inhabitants. If Miss Bradford's little house and little story delight children and challenge their imagination, and if they stimulate the memory or satisfy the intelligence of adults, they will have served their purpose.

WILCOMB E. WASHBURN
Director, Office of American Studies,
Smithsonian Institution

Library of Congress Cataloging in Publication Data
Bradford, Faith, 1880-1970.
The Dolls' house.
1. Doll-houses—Exhibitions. 2. National Museum of History and Technology. I. Title.
NK4892.U6W372 1976 745.59'23'0740153 77-179293
ISBN O-87474-283-8